"Are you stuck on doing a lifebook? Or scared to start a conversation about adoption with your child? Cindy Probst's fabulous book, *Adoption Lifebook: A Bridge to Your Child's Beginnings*, will inspire you to find the right path for you and your child. Cindy's honest, compassionate book, with suggestions from the hundreds of parents who have attended her ser nars, is a wise guide that enables parents to address adoption issues whil strengthening a child's self image."

> – *Shanti Fry, President, Families with Children from China-New England and the Foundation for Chinese Orphanages*

"Cindy Probst has crafted a sensitive and fact-filled guide to lifebooks which will be of immeasurable help to adoptive families."

> – *Mary Sullivan, Chair, Families for Russian and Ukrainian Adoption, New England Chapter*

"This book skillfully addresses many of the difficult issues that arise when one begins the creative task of writing a lifebook for the internationally adopted child. I look forward to sharing this book with friends."

> – *Kim DeAndrade, Guatemala Family Network*

"Cindy Probst has provided a workbook for international adoptive families to help them create a meaningful lifebook from the perspective of their child. KAAN is happy to share this resource with its families of Korean-born children."

> – *Chris Winston, Chair, Korean American, Adoptee, Adoptive Family Network*

"Create a gift that your adopted child will treasure for years to come with this thoughtful and practical guide. *Adoption Lifebook* propels you step by step through the writing process, integrating their adoption history into your child's unique story."

> – *Allison Martin, National Director, Families with Children from Vietnam*

ADOPTION LIFEBOOK

A BRIDGE TO YOUR CHILD'S BEGINNINGS

A WORKBOOK
FOR INTERNATIONAL
ADOPTIVE FAMILIES

By Cindy Probst, MEd, MSW, LCSW
Adoption Specialist, Adoptive Parent

Published by
BOSTON ADOPTION PRESS
POST OFFICE BOX 623
BOSTON, MA 02134

First published 2002
Second edition 2004
Third edition 2007

Printed in the United States of America

Library of Congress Catalog Number: 2002090091
ISBN: 978-0-9717496-0-3

THIS BOOK IS DEDICATED
TO MY CHILDREN,
TO ALL CHILDREN,
AND TO ALL OF THE PARENTS
THEY HOLD IN THEIR HEARTS.

ACKNOWLEDGMENTS

I N 1999, RIKA SMITH MCNALLY and Nancy Nies, board members of Families with Children from China-New England (FCC-NE), attended a lifebook workshop I offered at Concord Family and Youth Services. Subsequently, Rika and Nancy put to work their extraordinary talents to organize workshops for the community of FCC parents to learn about lifebooks. I was invited to be the social worker for these workshops. Among those who attended the earlier workshops were Jennifer Chen, Shelagh Ellman-Pearl, Jackie Farrell, Lisa King, Susan Ladd, and Maura Valle, who, together with Chairs Rika Smith McNally and Nancy Nies, became the FCC-NE Lifebook Project Team. Together we have envisioned a growing movement of parents who, through creating lifebooks, confidently welcome questions from and discussion with their children about their adoption backgrounds.

It takes a village for a book to happen, I have learned! I wish to thank the dedicated and skilled members of the Concord Family and Youth Services (CFYS) Adoption Team. Nancy H. Clayman, Director of Adoption, has been instrumental, both directly and indirectly, in the creation of this workbook. The CFYS team includes Carol Cataldo, Debbie Flanders, Hope Rubin, Carol Sheingold, Jean Sweeney, and Phyllis Terrey. I extend a special thank you to the parents and children I have professionally come to know who have shown me just how important a lifebook can be.

I am grateful for the support that Shanti Fry, president of FCC-NE, has extended to me, to the FCC-NE Lifebook Project, and to the community of parents who wish to share their children's beginnings with them in the form of a lifebook. Many special thanks to the adoption agencies, individuals from adoption travel groups, and representatives of FCC, Families for Russian and Ukrainian Adoption (FRUA), and others throughout the United States who have contacted me to inquire about lifebook workshops.

I extend special thanks to Annie, Gabriel, Jenia, Rebecca, Sara, Sasha, and Thea, whose portraits appear in the book. I also wish to recognize the following stars who are not pictured: Julie, Katherine, Sophie, and Tasha.

An extraordinary team of individuals came together to make this book happen. These talented professionals to whom I extend great thanks are Stephanie Faucher, designer; Susan Nicholl, editor; and Debra Samdperil, photographer.

This workbook is available to the community of adoptive families because of Rika Smith McNally. Rika has organized, coordinated, and guided each step of the production of this book. I am indebted to Rika for her exceptional commitment, expertise, vision, support, and belief in this project.

Joyce Colman, Eli Dan, Jennifer Dundon, Tim Dunn, Ann Duvall, Deborah Haynor, Judy Hunt, Amy Klatzkin, Nellie Loring, Renee Lubowich, Eileen McCluskey, John McDargh, John McNally, Margie Perse, Berit Pratt, Cal Probst, Lori Probst, Cheryl Schaffer, Jan Simon, Betsy Smith, Ellen Weisstein, Jodie Wigren, and the Blueberry Cove campers and their parents have in many ways made valuable contributions to this workbook. I would especially like to recognize Jackie Farrell and Nancy Nies for their wisdom, energy, and encouragement, Susan Avery for her perspective and generosity, and Melissa Probst and Sue Pearce for their boundless support and unwavering belief in me. I cannot thank them enough.

I am especially grateful to the parents and waiting parents who have participated in the lifebook workshops – who, together with my own family, have guided me here.

Here it is, Dad.

PREFACE TO THE THIRD EDITION

The reception for *Adoption Lifebook: A Bridge to Your Child's Beginnings*, by the community of adoptive families, waiting parents, and adoption professionals, has been extraordinary. Thank you to all of the individuals, travel groups, agencies, and organizations who continue to enthusiastically support this project.

The parents and waiting parents who organize and participate in lifebook sessions continue to energize my thinking and lead me to reflect again and again on the passion and spirit of this community. Individually and collectively, we are empowering ourselves to share in our children's stories with them, and passing that strength and confidence on to them. I am grateful for the opportunity to share in this movement with you all.

Since *Adoption Lifebook: A Bridge to Your Child's Beginnings* was first published, I have continually been reminded how much of a difference a lifebook can make. May it fill your hearts as it does mine to consider this generation of strong, resilient children who know who they are, and the bridges they are building to the future!

Cindy Probst
2007

For my wonderful family,
for whom I am endlessly bursting with love and pride.

CONTENTS

INTRODUCTION

ADOPTIVE PARENTS hold in their hearts precious bits of information about the earliest days, months, or years of their children's lives, before they joined their families. Parents understand this information is invaluable to their children, yet they wonder how to share it with them. "Is it all right to tell her she was abandoned?" "Do I need to talk about her birth parents? If so, how?" "Can I stretch the truth or leave out painful truths?" "What can I say when I know so little?"

This workbook is designed for parents who wish to sensitively and honestly document the facts and circumstances of their children's early lives for them, in the enduring form of a lifebook. For parents who are unsure of where or how to begin this effort, or who feel stuck in the process of recording their child's history, here you will find useful suggestions and step-by-step help along the way.

Why go to the trouble of creating a lifebook for your child?

It may take some courage to pick up this workbook. It can be difficult to contemplate sharing with our children the stories of their early lives that do not include us. This workbook does not propose an "easy way" to write a lifebook. The emphasis here is not merely on getting it done but rather on communicating effectively and thoughtfully with our children about their backgrounds. Whether your children are from China, South Korea, Guatemala, Russia, Ethiopia, Kazakhstan, Ukraine, or another country, by writing a lifebook you are actively contributing to their emotional well-being by shaping how they will view their beginnings.

Composing a lifebook does take thought and effort. We choose to create lifebooks so our children will have the best chance to feel as good as they can about themselves. When parents make these investments of time and energy, children can draw on this information whenever they want to for the rest of their lives.

In this workbook you will find ideas and exercises to help you conceptualize and create a lifebook for your child. Direction is offered on subjects that parents tend to find most challenging, such as what to include, how to phrase sad or painful information, how to approach the concept of birth parents, how to address our own feelings as we encounter the material, and how lifebooks may be used. For linguistic ease, children are referred to as "she," rather than "he/she." Details have been altered to protect the anonymity of families presented in some of the examples.

As the community of international adoptive families has grown, so too has interest in lifebooks. Parents enthusiastically seek guidance from adoptive family organizations, adoption agencies, and each other to create lifebooks for their children. Through lifebook workshops offered specifically to international adoptive families, I have had the privilege of meeting with and learning from hundreds of parents who have generously shared their feelings, thoughts, and stories. My vision for this book arose, in part, from these stimulating sessions.

In lifebook workshops, I share with parents my belief that the stories of children's beginnings belong to the children. I offer reassurance that one need not be creative nor a writer in order to create a lifebook, and together we brainstorm what to say and how to phrase it for the children. I am always moved by the intense level of interest in the topic, the depth of feeling put forth by group members, and burdens lifted from parents for whom a bit of information resonated.

In the workshops, I highlight four main ideas that underscore this approach to lifebooks:

1. Adoptive families are one of many healthy and strong variations of family.
2. The most important step in creating a lifebook is reframing the information to emphasize the child's

strengths and resilience while maintaining its truthfulness.

3. During the process of creating their children's lifebooks, parents decide how they will share certain information with their children. Parents who once felt nervous just anticipating such conversations with their children now feel stronger and more confident in these discussions.

4. Parents are encouraged to look to the wisdom and support of other adoptive parents.

Through my work as an adoption specialist, I have learned that parents usually do intend to share the stories of their children's early lives with them but often are unsure about how to proceed. Parents worry about "hurting their feelings," "making them feel sad," or "saying the wrong thing." As an adoptive parent, I understand and relate to these feelings. My intent is for workbook readers, as for workshop participants, to feel more comfortable and competent sharing with their children in the stories of their beginnings. Children then learn their own histories from parents who are more confident and able to share the truth, yet who can emphasize their children's strengths and resilience under difficult circumstances.

Creating lifebooks for our children is a process, with stops and starts along the way. The process itself is part of the journey. I hope the journey to your child's lifebook is a fulfilling one.

> "I WISH MY PARENTS HAD MADE A LIFEBOOK FOR ME.
> EVEN THOUGH THEY DIDN'T KNOW MUCH ABOUT
> MY PAST, IT WOULD HAVE HELPED ME BETTER
> UNDERSTAND WHO I AM AND WHERE I CAME FROM."
> – Melinda, age 29

CHAPTER 1

What Is a Lifebook?

WHAT IS A LIFEBOOK?

OUR CHILDREN EXIST before we meet, no matter how young they are when we become family. This is a given of adoption. Lifebooks simply offer a way to document their lives before we came into the picture. Through text and usually some pictures, too, lifebooks tell their stories from their points of view. Lifebooks allow us to share the facts, however few we have, sensitively and honestly, to help our children understand their beginnings.

Lifebooks were originally created for children who moved from one state foster home to another. They were written to help children understand where they had lived and with whom, and why their moves had occurred. Over time the lifebook concept has been adapted for children from a wide range of adoption backgrounds.

The child's point of view

A lifebook is created for, about, and from the perspective of the child. It answers such questions as, "What do you know about my early life?" and "How and why did I come to be adopted?" This seemingly easy concept can actually be quite difficult to put into practice. As Jayne, a lifebook workshop participant, put it, "How can I think about Adam's life before I was in it?"

Some of us have experienced disappointments associated with infertility.

Some of us longed to be parents for many years. The arrival of our child may have made our dreams come true. But a lifebook tells the *child's own* story. These important aspects of our paths to parenthood are not part of our children's journeys; our journey to parenthood can be recorded elsewhere.

The emotional landscape

Many adoptive parents have reported their intent to create lifebooks for their children: they gather their information and sit amid airplane ticket stubs and trip photos, unsure where or how to begin. For some, the emotional landscape may seem daunting. Perhaps it feels surprisingly difficult to say or write the phrase "birth mother." Feelings related to infertility, once thought to be resolved, may unexpectedly arise. Or how does one write that one's child was placed on a street corner, or that her birth family lived in poverty?

Some parents find it healing to tune into their own feelings about their child's early life experience while composing her lifebook. We can then privately honor our own feelings without "giving" our feelings to our children. Later, when sharing with our children in the story of their early lives, we are better able to be emotionally present and available to them rather than caught in our own feelings about the material.

A lifebook need not be fancy

There is much room for variation in a lifebook: take from here the ideas that work for you. My point of view can be found throughout. Lifebooks may be written by hand or typed; some include photos, drawings, maps, or stickers. Some children participate in the creation of theirs. Some lifebooks are simple, and some are elaborate. A simple three-ring binder with plastic page protectors can be quite suitable. To discover what works for your family, consider your personal style and the personality of your child. To help you determine how to create it, imagine how your child may use her lifebook in the future.

While the term *lifebook* is widely used, some families will prefer to label a child's completed book with a personal title that relates to their child, such as *Rachel: My First Ten Months*.

As for the photographs, ticket stubs, and memorabilia that are not part of your child's lifebook – you might want to consider an album for those precious photos and a separate special scrapbook for the wealth of mementos (reported by many to occupy a box in the closet!) collected on your trip.

Why create a lifebook?

"I WAS BORN FROM AN AIRPLANE."
– *Michael, age 5*

The primary purpose of a lifebook is for your child to have access to the facts of her life before joining your family. A lifebook is documentation of your child's past – written confirmation that she has had one. She, too, grew inside a woman's womb and was born.

Even a small bit of knowledge about your child's early history reduces her uncertainty. Children who do not have information still have questions; it is not unusual for adopted children to fabricate their own explanations for the missing pieces of their stories. Some children actually believe they "came from" airplanes. Your child's airport arrival may be the point at which she became "real" for you. Perhaps, as for many of us, you wish her life began when you became her parent/s. But our children's lives began elsewhere – and without us. This is their truth. While they are very young we hold it, but it belongs to them. Though not comprehensive, lifebooks are our best attempts to provide written documentation of our children's beginnings to assist them on their personal paths to greater self-understanding.

In addition to being a written source of information, lifebooks offer an effective vehicle for discussion. Talking with our children about adoption is healthy and necessary. Opportunities to talk about it arise spontaneously, especially when we are open to recognizing them. Rebecca, a workshop participant, viewed her neighbor's pregnancy as an opportunity to clarify with her daughter that she, too, grew inside a woman's womb, that that woman is her birth mother, and that she also has a birth father.

Even though a lifebook is written from the child's point of view, looking first at our own life experience can help us better understand the perspective of our children – to let us "walk in their shoes," so to speak.

Your own birth

Part 1: Do you know where were you were born? Do you know your birth weight? What details do you have of your parents' experience of your birth? Are you aware of reactions of siblings or feelings of extended family members to your birth? Do you know your true date of birth? Write the first memories that come to you.

_____

_____

_____

_____

_____

_____

_____

_____

_____

_____

_____

_____

_____

_____

_____

_____

Part 2: How would your life be different if you had not had access to this information? If this information is not available to you, what would be different if you had had this knowledge?

_____

_____

_____

_____

_____

_____

_____

_____

_____

Lifebooks vary, of course, depending on individual preferences and families' styles. Some families have chosen to include definitions of relevant words that the child is likely to hear to help her understand how these words may or may not apply to her. Such words could be *abandoned, orphan,* or *foundling,* for example. She can then turn back again and again, as her level of sophistication changes, to reintegrate those definitions into her greater understanding of herself and her beginnings.

A frequently overlooked benefit of preparing a lifebook is the comfort level parents reach while writing and rewriting aspects of their child's history. Once the writer feels satisfied with a particular section, he or she likely has spent a long time processing that bit of information and feels better prepared to discuss it with the child when the time comes.

For some two-parent families, preparing their child's lifebook becomes an opportunity to share individual viewpoints regarding the child's background and to discuss how they will present it to their child. One parent remarked, "For David and me, the lifebook process gave us more opportunity to discuss and come to a meeting of the minds on approaches to the terminology of adoption and other areas where we've had different opinions."

CHAPTER 2

Getting Started

GETTING STARTED

EXERCISE 2 · *Jotting It All Down*

Briefly jot down the basic information that you intend to include in your child's lifebook. Note simple facts, without emphasis on phrasing; this part is just to help you prepare for writing. It may be helpful to do this sooner rather than later, even if you do not plan to write the text now. The details may seem less crisp with time, and it may be harder to come up with descriptions.

Include such information as your knowledge of your child's birth parents and birth siblings, orphanage caretakers, foster family, any moves, health, and reasons leading to her adoption. For more ideas, refer to examples of questions children may have on page 32.

EXERCISE 3 · *Figuring Out What to Include*

In addition to the previous information, what do you imagine your child will wish to know about her earliest days, months, or years? What questions do you hope to answer for her in this lifebook? Even though you will not have the answers to all – or even some – of them, it can be helpful to keep these questions in mind while writing.

CHILDREN MAY HAVE THESE SORTS OF QUESTIONS

1. Was I born?
2. Why couldn't my birth parents raise me?
3. How and when did I get from my birth parents to the orphanage, foster parents, or other caretakers?
4. Who gave me my name?
5. What type of area or community did I live in?
6. With whom did I live? Who took care of me? What were their names?
7. What did my home look like? Did I share a room, crib, or bed?
8. What was my life like? What was my daily routine? What was my general health? What skills had I developed? Did I have any special friends? What were my favorite toys or foods? Do you know someone who has since traveled there who may have photos or additional information?
9. Why was I not adopted sooner? (if your child was older)
10. Where and how was my special need diagnosed? What kinds of special services or help, if any, did I receive?
11. Is my medical condition common in my country of origin?
12. How did I acquire this scar?
13. Is my birthdate actual or estimated?
14. Do I have biologically related siblings?
15. Did my birth parents die?

EXERCISE 4 · *For Waiting Parents*

Waiting parents who travel have the opportunity, prior to their trips, to formulate questions that their children might have about their origins as they grow up. Consider in advance how you might collect this information. Talk with other adoptive parents about information they or their children wish they had. Learn how they found information that was helpful to their child. Is it possible for you to visit your child's birth parents, foster parents, other relatives, or people who cared for your child? Can you visit your child's birthplace, the village, town, or city where your child was born, or the site where she was placed?

Prior to your trip, compose a list of questions about your child's early life. Emphasize questions relating to her background, such as when she arrived at the orphanage or foster home and who took care of her there, rather than her routine (such as her present sleep schedule, which is going to be disrupted anyway). Try to anticipate the questions your child may have in the future (see Exercise 3). Exercising cultural sensitivity (see box below), gather as much relevant information for your child during your trip as you are able. One good tip while traveling: While you're awake at night, in between trips to court or the consulate or waiting for a plane, write it all down!

A TRAVEL TIP

What is considered respectful behavior varies in each culture. Prior to your trip, try to learn about these cultural differences. Do individuals engage in eye contact? Is there a slower, more relaxed pace that you are not used to? What is an effective approach to accessing the information you are seeking that respects the values of the local people? Knowing the answers before you travel may help you adapt your behavior more easily once you arrive.

EXERCISE 5 · *Composing Your Outline*

Put together a general outline based on the information you have compiled (in Exercise 2) and the questions you hope to address (from Exercise 3). Remember to include the broader context of your child's adoption circumstances – the greater social, political, and/or economic realities that serve as a backdrop to her birth parents' decision. This important information, to which she will likely turn again and again, relates to the question, "Why was I adopted?"

This example provides a broader context:

- IN THE COUNTRYSIDE OF CAMBODIA, FEW JOBS PAY VERY MUCH MONEY. SOMETIMES THERE ISN'T ENOUGH MONEY FOR PARENTS TO BUY IMPORTANT THINGS, LIKE ENOUGH FOOD OR CLOTHES, WHICH ALL FAMILIES NEED. ALL PARENTS WANT THEIR CHILDREN TO HAVE GOOD LIVES WITH THESE NECESSARY THINGS.

Here are some other examples:

- MY BIRTH MOTHER AND BIRTH FATHER WERE NOT MARRIED. BIRTH MOTHERS AND BIRTH FATHERS ARE NOT WELCOME TO RAISE THEIR CHILDREN IF THEY ARE NOT MARRIED. PEOPLE FEEL SAD ABOUT THIS CUSTOM BECAUSE THEY LOVE CHILDREN SO MUCH.
- ALL COUNTRIES HAVE RULES. IN CHINA THERE ARE RULES ABOUT HAVING CHILDREN. MORE PEOPLE LIVE IN CHINA THAN IN ANY OTHER COUNTRY IN THE WORLD. THE PEOPLE IN CHARGE ARE WORRIED THAT THERE WON'T BE ENOUGH FOOD, HOUSING AND OTHER THINGS PEOPLE NEED IF FAMILIES HAVE MANY CHILDREN – SO THEY MADE A RULE TO LIMIT THE SIZE OF FAMILIES.
- IN SOME VILLAGES IN ETHIOPIA, FAMILIES MAY NOT HAVE ENOUGH MONEY TO BUY FOOD AND OTHER THINGS ALL CHILDREN NEED. IT MAY BE THAT PARENTS EARN SOME MONEY, BUT NOT ENOUGH FOR ALL OF THEIR CHILDREN TO HAVE HEALTHY LIVES. OR THERE MAY NOT BE ENOUGH MONEY FOR A FAMILY BECAUSE A PARENT MAY BE VERY ILL OR MAY HAVE DIED. FRIENDS AND RELATIVES IN THE VILLAGES TRY TO HELP EACH OTHER.

For another example, see page 55.

Obtaining more information

In every lifebook workshop, parents wish they had more information for their children. "We didn't know what to ask" and "We were so caught up in the moment!" are among the most common remarks. Some of them have not let distance, access, differences in language, or the passage of time limit their ability to keep trying! In other words, for those who are inclined, it's never too late to try to obtain more information.

Some parents, while being careful to respect the cultural system, have written letters to former foster parents or orphanage caretakers asking specific questions about their children. Another has contacted someone in the region where the child was born who agreed to take photos of the area for the family. In Cambodia, some adoptive parents hired an individual to sensitively explore a child's background. Parents have accessed Internet websites that pertain to certain countries or particular orphanages. New families returning from China have brought new information to families of children who once lived at the same orphanage. Some individuals have returned to Korea to investigate their own beginnings. A number of parents have successfully received information about the birth families of their children in Guatemala with the assistance of a particular social worker there.

I've read of one family's return to China to visit the child's foster family: through networking, this family was able to trace the individual in whose yard the baby had been placed who subsequently brought her to the orphanage. Another family keeps in touch with their child's orphanage caretaker in Russia. Through adoptive family connections, a teenage boy has learned some new information about his beginnings in Colombia. With each story, my heart is warmed by the lengths to which some parents extend themselves and the creativity involved to acquire even the slightest bit of information for their children. This little fragment of information could be a most significant tidbit to a child!

The age level of your child's lifebook

"MY SON IS THREE YEARS OLD. HOW DO I
MAKE A LIFEBOOK FOR A YOUNG CHILD?"

While preparing your child's lifebook, you may find it useful to have a target age in mind. That is, aim for a particular level of sophistication in terms of content, language, and presentation. (You may want to consider that many children are asking questions at age three and looking at their identities especially around age ten.) The text can be revised with your child as she grows. You may also choose to make changes in your child's lifebook as your thoughts become more refined, as you come to know your child at her "target age," and/or as you acquire new information.

A younger child, a child who needs help to pay attention, or a child who functions at a young cognitive level is likely to respond more positively to a visually appealing book that includes a greater number of photographs or other visual materials (such as maps or pictures photocopied from books). A nine- or ten-year-old is typically better able to understand abstraction and distinguish between fact and speculation, so her lifebook would rely predominantly on the text.

Parents of younger children have generally found it easier to create the first draft of the more sophisticated "older child" version first, and then draw from this material to make a simpler version for a younger child. The reverse – generating the more inclusive version from the simpler one (when the information is not as fresh in your mind) – can be a greater challenge.

Keep in mind that all available information relevant to a child's beginnings is typically included in a lifebook. If a particular circumstance is not developmentally appropriate to include, such as conception through violence, you may choose to consult professionals about how and when to share that material with your child. My belief is that a child should not learn of such information for the first time in a lifebook. Such circumstances might be implied in one's lifebook in order to keep the lifebook truthful and to generate discussion.

By disclosing all of what we know, our children are more likely to trust what we do share and understand that we are not keeping any knowledge from them. We are increasing their opportunities for growing and healing.

EXERCISE 6 · *Preparing to Write*

Imagine yourself in the village, city, or province of your child's birth. What does the landscape look like? What are the smells and sounds? What is the pace? What are people doing in the markets, streets, or fields? What do dwellings look like? How are people dressed? Do you see crowds of people? Traffic? Animals? People walking? People riding bicycles?

How might you transfer some of these images, which are so relevant to your child's early life, to your lifebook pages? Try to use some of these descriptions in your writing to accurately set the stage for the larger societal issues that have affected your child's birth parents. For example, if her birth parents are unable to parent because they live in poverty, as is the situation for many birth parents in Brazil, Ecuador, Guatemala, India, Romania, Russia, Vietnam, and elsewhere, you may want to sensitively report signs of poverty there. In China, rules designed to limit population growth severely constrain birth parents' freedom to choose to raise a child. You may wish to draw attention to the large population by noting crowds of people there. This can help begin to establish for your child the circumstances that are greater than her birth parents that led to their decision not to raise her.

You may choose to begin your child's lifebook with an anecdote, or you may start with your child's name and place of birth or offer some background about your child's country of origin. Each lifebook is unique. In general, it is probably easiest for a child to follow a book that moves along chronologically.

- MY NAME IS STEPHEN BENJAMIN MURPHY. I LIVE IN PHILADELPHIA, PENNSYLVANIA, USA. I HAVEN'T ALWAYS LIVED IN PENNSYLVANIA. I WAS BORN IN NOVOSIBIRSK, RUSSIA.

While reconstructing your child's story for her, try to offer whatever details you can. If you had the opportunity to visit her home, orphanage, or birthplace, include a description of the building, room, or garden. If you were able to meet the orphanage director, a caretaker, or someone who knew your child at that time, include names, if possible, and describe their appearances. These re-creations can help her visualize her early environment.

What to write, how to write?

Parents are usually surprised to find that they have more information about their child's background than originally suspected. This type of information is sometimes not obvious until you've started to think about it. Consider, for example, the weather in your child's place of birth at the time of year she was born. What clothing is worn there during that season? Are most people farmers? Factory workers? When you include information of this sort in your child's lifebook, be sure to distinguish between the information you know for sure and your educated guesses (*see page 65*).

One mom shared with me a heartfelt letter written by her daughter's foster family at the time of the girl's adoption at age three. In it, her foster family offered love and blessings for her in her new family. Gifts such as this extraordinary letter are not common. Should you possess a comment, note, or letter given to you by a birth parent, foster parent, or caretaker that pertains to your child's beginnings, consider including a copy of it in your child's lifebook.

If your child was adopted at an older age, be sure to include the memories she has shared with you of her life before her adoption. One child, who was three years old when she was adopted, has talked about her memories of her separation from her birth mother. Gently encourage your child to recall details. For example, if she talks about a particular room, does she remember any color or decoration on the walls? If she remembers a special outing, can she tell you how or with whom she traveled? She may be able to tell you now about an invaluable detail, smell, or sound that years from now will no longer be consciously remembered. Be sure to write it down.

In a lifebook workshop with parents of children born in Russia, Ukraine, Colombia, and China, Sara proposed a common question: "My five-year-old son says he is from Ukraine. At this point, do I need to tell him more about his early life?" Children build upon information already in their possession. As we plant seeds of information, we help increase their readiness for subsequent information; we "set the stage," so to speak. What seeds do we plant here with the hope of greater future understanding? This can be a useful framework to keep in mind while composing the lifebook text.

The tone of the document is largely influenced, of course, by the words we choose to use. Opinions differ about how to refer to the child whose story is being told. One suggestion is to word it in the second person, referring to the child as *you*. If you expect your child to be reading independently when she reaches the age you have targeted, then my suggestion is to use the first person. In the initial draft of my older daughter's book, she was identified by the pronoun *you*. I now realize how much easier it was for *me* to have that distance. Once she was reading on her own, she requested a change to the pronouns *I* and *me*, which offered a less insulated and direct tone. Creating a lifebook is an ongoing process, one that adapts to the changing needs and comprehension of your child. Again, consider what feels right for your child.

Word choices are so important. Words can be constructive and contribute to one's well-being or be harmful and damaging. The adoption language we use at home is the language with which our children become most familiar. They hear these words first and most often from us. Our word choices can contribute to our children's feelings about adoption and about themselves.

Certain words convey stronger, more positive adoption messages than other terms do. *Birth mother*, *birth father*, and *birth parents* are accurately descriptive terms. Referring to a child's birth mother as her *Russian mother* may imply an ongoing parenting relationship that may feel confusing to a child.

Some examples:
- They were not able to *parent* or *raise* (rather than *keep*) you.
- They *made an adoption plan* or a *decision* (rather than *gave you up* or *put you up* for adoption).
- You were *placed* (rather than *left*) on a busy street corner.
- *We became family* or *she arrived* (rather than we *got* her) in December.
- Consider sometimes saying *we are an adoptive family* rather than *she was adopted* to place the focus on the family rather than the child.
- Consider using the term *sponsor* (rather than *adopt*) for objects, animals, highways, and programs.

- Our children generally do not hear references to their births as do children who were not adopted. Using the phrase *before you were born* when referring to past events – perhaps just hearing the word *born* refer to them – can affirm that they were born just like everyone else. "We saw that movie a long time ago, before you were born," or "That happened before you were born," for example.

As with everything else, our children pick up on our attitudes toward adoption. If adoption is presented to young children in a positive light, they are likely to view it as positive. We and our children are strengthened when we see our children as resilient and our families as one of many variations of family.

CHAPTER 3

The Challenges of Writing

CHALLENGES OF WRITING

Difficult information

To be most useful to your child, a lifebook should include all information about her life before you met that is developmentally appropriate and specific to her. As stated earlier, in addition to her own individual story, this includes the greater social, economic, and political context of her birth country that is relevant to her individual circumstances. It also includes reasons not specific to her individual birth parents that "explain" why her parents were unable to raise her (poverty, societal gender preference, societal views of single parent-hood, war, one son/two child policy, death of birth parents, etc).

For example, you might write:

- THROUGHOUT THEIR LIVES, PEOPLE ARE TAUGHT THAT WHEN THEY ARE GROWN-UPS THEY MUST BE THE PARENTS OF A SON. THESE RULES PUT EXTRAORDINARY PRESSURE ON CHINESE FAMILIES, WHO DEEPLY LOVE THEIR DAUGHTERS BUT BELIEVE THEY MUST PARENT A SON.

Turn back to page 40 for more examples.

It can seem that our children's lives began when we became family. One of the gifts of a lifebook is the acknowledgment in writing for our children that they, indeed, were born. You may not possess many facts of your child's birth, such as her birth weight or place of birth. You do know, however, that she has a birth mother and a birth father. You do know that her birth mother was pregnant with her. What information do you have about women in the city, town, village, or province of her birth? Is there anything you have learned that you suspect is a likely scenario for her birth parents? Were they most likely married? Is it likely that her birth mother continued to work during her pregnancy?

If a certain scenario is highly likely, it is acceptable to include it in the text as "highly likely." This information can help your child create a picture in her mind of her birth parents as real people. Most adoption professionals explain that it is easier for a person to feel rooted and, therefore, navigate forward more smoothly if she understands that her birth parents and early history are real. This does not mean, however, that without this understanding one is destined to have more difficulty.

The following sections address how to present information honestly and sensitively. Walk in your child's shoes while composing the text. Remember that the purpose of the lifebook is not to celebrate you as a family, but rather to set the stage for your child and assist in her self-understanding.

Our own issues

Some parents report feeling stuck while putting together their children's lifebooks; others feel tearful while writing. For some, documenting the material is fairly straightforward.

For some individuals, especially those who have experienced infertility, writing the text can be a painful reminder that we are not, in fact, the biological parents of our children. One mom tearfully shared her belief that she was a disappointment to her daughter because she was unable to breastfeed her.

Contemplating our children's birth parents or births can raise feelings about our own losses. Writing the words *birth mother* or *birth father* can make birth parents real to us, perhaps for the first time.

While compiling the material, some parents feel sad when remembering their children's personal experiences. It can be hard to imagine our children's former circumstances, depending on the nature of their situations.

In lifebook groups, many have shared their sadness over children whom they had grown to love through adoption referral pictures and intended to parent, yet, due to a variety of circumstances, the adoption did not work out. A majority of these parents, to whom another child was presented right away, have not since had the opportunity to address their own feelings about the loss of the first child. For some, feelings about these first children have arisen as they have prepared to compose their children's lifebooks. Parents have wondered if perhaps this information ought to be included in lifebooks. These losses and experiences are significant aspects of *our* journeys as parents, but not of our children's paths. Consider sharing your story with your child later, when she is developmentally ready.

Helen becomes teary every time her daughter, Maya, asks a question about her adoption. Maya felt that she was making her mom upset, so she stopped asking about her past. If preparing your child's lifebook taps into your personal losses or otherwise produces feelings of sadness, consider taking a break and allowing yourself those feelings. Putting together a lifebook can contribute to one's own healing.

Birth parents

Our children typically have very limited information about their birth parents. It is expected and healthy for them to try to identify with their birth parents at some level, and we can help our children add some depth to this knowledge.

Simply responding to your child's question, "How tall do you think I will grow?" with a response that relates to her birth parents, such as, "Perhaps you will be as tall as your birth mother," reinforces that her birth mother is a real person with whom she can identify. Attributing a child's special interest or skill to that of a birth parent can also reinforce this positive view. You might say, "You are so good at ____. I wonder if you got that from your birth parents."

Qualities that may be biologically determined, such as hand dominance, can be another avenue for facilitating that identification: "You are left-handed. Your birth mother or birth father may be left-handed, too."

"WILL ACKNOWLEDGMENT OF MY DAUGHTER'S BIRTH FATHER
MAKE HER FEEL BAD ABOUT HAVING A SINGLE MOM?"

In lifebook workshops, some single parents and parents in families with two moms or two dads report that their children have found references to the birth parent whose gender differs from the adoptive parent(s) to be especially welcome and of special interest.

A PLACE FOR BIRTH PARENTS

We are our children's parents. We listen to their wishes and dreams. We share in their joys, disappointments, and growing up. We teach them our values. We help shape their behavior. We prepare their meals, scramble to get them off to daycare or school, and are up with them during the night. Our children know us as such.

We are not our children's birth parents. We were not pregnant with them. We did not give birth to them. We share neither their birth family history nor a genetic past with them. These parts of our children's lives are shared with their birth parents.

Our children's birth families are part of who they are, with or without distance and information. If we honor the birth parents' places in our children's lives, by helping our children identify with the feeling of them, perhaps our children will be better equipped to feel good about the whole of their identities.

Parents may suppose that talking about birth parents raises sad feelings for children. In order to shield them from this, parents may choose not to speak about birth parents. However, children know they have birth parents. Is our silence received by them as an unspoken message that their birth parents are "bad" and shouldn't be spoken about? Is it possible that children then identify themselves as "bad," since this may be the only thing they "know" about them?

If you are aware of any personal insecurity related to your child's birth parents, it can help to be in touch with it. Does it affect your confidence as a parent? Do you have fears that your child will love her birth parents more than she loves you? Experiences of infertility? Worries about saying the "wrong" thing?

Your child is likely to receive your positive and honest portrayal of her birth parents (and her country and culture of origin) in part as messages about her. Accepting and honoring your child's birth parents does not diminish your definition as parent. Rather, you are able to claim the whole of your child.

EXERCISE 8 · *Thinking About Birth Parents*

Close your eyes and think about your child's birth mother and birth father. You may or may not have met them. How do you or might you honor their place in your child's life? How might you help your child identify with them and her culture of origin in a positive way?

_____

_____

_____

_____

_____

_____

_____

_____

_____

_____

_____

_____

On Difference

Providing Children With Positive Messages About Adoptive Families

Our culture teaches us that adoption is a method of becoming parents, an avenue to parenthood, a means to an end. Our expectation may then be that once a child joins our family, our family is the same as others.

All families, of course, are different. Each family operates in its own particular ways depending on such factors as race, ethnicity, religion, ability, age, gender, and a host of other differences and factors. Adoptive families also are different.

The larger culture teaches us to view such differences as negative. We and our children learn from television, videos, movies, magazines, and advertisers to value being thin and able; having light skin, hair, and eyes; having a mother and a father whom we resemble; and solving problems in thirty minutes (or seconds, in the case of commercials). We do not generally see positive images of multiracial or multicultural adoptive families reflected in the mainstream media.

Our children see themselves as different from those they see in the media. They may internalize the negative messages about differences to which they are exposed every day. We want our children to feel proud of who they are. It is important for us, then, to provide them with positive messages not only about adoption, but also about people representing all kinds of diversity.

Many international adoptive families integrate into their lives elements of the culture of their child's country of origin. Treasured items from the country are displayed throughout the home, not only in the bedroom of the child. This small gesture demonstrates the family's recognition of the child's culture as part of their own and reinforces her sense of belonging.

Adoptive parents arrange language classes, after-school culture programs, culture camps, playgroups, newsletters, and travel group reunions. Some families participate in intensive language training programs while living with host families in other countries. Organizations such as Adoptive Families Together (AFT); Ethiopian Kids Community (EKC); Families with Cambodian Children (FamCam); Families with Children from China (FCC); Families for Russian and Ukrainian Adoption (FRUA); Families with Children from Vietnam (FCV); Korean American, Adoptee, Adoptive Family Network (KAAN); Latin American Adoptive Families (LAAF); Open Door Society; and many others provide education and organize events and social activities. Online groups have become another option for adoptive family networking. Some families participate in cultural festivals, holidays, and community celebrations. For many, these connections with other adoptive families are a priority.

Through these networks, adoptive families socialize, exchange ideas, and support one another. Parents share the joys of parenting as well as their experiences responding to intrusive questions, racism, and stereotypes. They discuss the school programs that are most receptive to adoptive families and those with greater racial and cultural diversity. They talk about teaching their kids to feel good about themselves when they are exposed to hurtful comments and behaviors based on cultural messages which are not inclusive, and they share resources with one another.

As well, parents are able to look to each other as children express thoughts related to feelings about their beginnings. They share their questions and feelings with others who understand and hope their children, when they are ready, will turn to each other in the same way.

So, in some ways, adoptive family life *is* different. We develop our own traditions, programs, and networks. We try to help our children feel good about the whole of who they are. We can model for them our pride in our differences (as an adoptive multiracial single-parent family, for example), and we demonstrate positive attitudes toward other "different" families and individuals and learn from each other.

And by doing so, we challenge messages in society which might otherwise undermine our own attitudes, values, and behaviors, and we create alternative concepts for our children.

How to say it

The *presentation* of the material, of course, is very important. What feelings and messages do you wish to convey in the text about your child's birth country, birth parents, or personality? What feeling or thought do you want each sentence to evoke in three, five, or ten years?

For example, you might want to write:

- Surely, most people in China feel sad about this rule because they love and care about children very much.
- Sometimes my birth father hit my birth mother when he was angry. He used his body to show his feelings. I know his behavior was wrong.

While offering hard information, these examples present empowering messages that remove from the child the responsibility for the reasons for her adoption.

Convey whatever *details* you can. It is these details which individualize the children's stories and make each personal, unique, and real. Children are often drawn to a simple detail that strikes them as particularly meaningful.

- Colorful cloth diapers hang outside on the porch to dry.
- Each baby has her own small, white crib cushioned with a straw mat to keep her cool in the warmer months.

Universalize concepts when possible. This can help children identify which aspects of their stories are particular to them and which pertain to others with similar circumstances.

- THIS PART OF MY EARLY LIFE IS VERY SIMILAR TO OTHER CHILDREN WHO WERE BORN IN KOREA AND HAVE ADOPTIVE FAMILIES.

In lifebook workshops, I am frequently asked whether children ought to be told if there is a question regarding the accuracy of their dates of birth. This information is part of their stories. And just like other aspects of their stories, this truth belongs to them.

- WE WERE TOLD THAT THE ORPHANAGE PEDIATRICIAN, JUDGING BY YOUR SIZE AND DEVELOPMENT (SUCH AS YOUR REFLEXES AND THE APPEARANCE OF YOUR BELLY BUTTON), CAREFULLY ESTIMATED YOUR AGE TO BE SIX DAYS OLD, AND YOUR BIRTHDATE, THEREFORE, TO BE JULY 21. IT IS POSSIBLE THAT THIS DATE IS NOT EXACTLY ACCURATE. MOST CHILDREN WHO WERE BORN IN CHINA AND WERE ADOPTED HAVE HAD THEIR BIRTHDATES ESTIMATED.

Be *honest*. Do not say she was the most beautiful baby in the orphanage unless you know it to be true (of course she was!). Use words such as *probably*, *most likely*, *surely*, or *maybe* when you are not certain.

- HOSPITALS ARE FAR AWAY FROM THE VILLAGE. CHILDREN WHO LIVE IN THIS AREA ARE BORN AT HOME, SO YOU WERE *PROBABLY* BORN AT HOME.

Equipped with the truth as best as we are able to provide, our children have the power to claim their own beginnings.

Positive reframing: fostering strength and resiliency in our children

"HOW DO I SENSITIVELY PRESENT THE
HARD PARTS OF HER BACKGROUND?"

When we present our children with information about their lives, we try to create a context for them. This approach differs from sharing their information with them shaded by our own points of reference. We want to present the facts neutrally so they can develop their own feelings about them.

Similarly, we want to be aware of the cultural lens through which we view our children's early circumstances. A particular practice may seem perfectly reasonable within one culture and very unfamiliar, or perhaps even "wrong" within another. These dilemmas come up for parents regularly in lifebook groups. For example, one parent, concerned that her toddler had spent too much time sitting on the potty in China, wondered how to tell her child about this perceived hard truth. Others in the group pointed out that this is a typical practice there, even though it is not the custom in the United States. We want to try not to skew our presentation to our children based on our own cultural experiences and biases.

The goal is to present your child's story, truthfully and sensitively, with emphasis on the personal strengths she, or her birth parents on her behalf, demonstrated in her particular situation. Positive reframing is important because the lifebook helps to create a foundation that will influence your child's feelings about her beginnings. There is a greater likelihood that she will view herself from a place of strength as she envisions her early life, I believe, if the information is shared with her from this positive perspective.

Consider an example. Suppose your child, not expected to survive, was neglected by the orphanage, or was abandoned on a street corner, in a hospital, or in a field. These stories can be painful for parents, who so love their children, to contemplate. How might this information be presented for your child in her lifebook?

Let's consider your child's strengths because it is her strengths which enabled her to survive. Did she cry with so much determination that passersby were forced to take notice? Did she take care of herself by using her strong voice and strength of spirit to get her needs met? The idea is to thoughtfully and accurately draw on the particular strengths of your child in her particular situation.

- I WAS VERY SICK WHEN I WAS A YOUNG BABY. I CRIED A LOT BECAUSE I DIDN'T FEEL WELL. MY PARENTS WERE TOLD THAT WHEN I CRIED I RECEIVED EXTRA ATTENTION. I USED MY POWERFUL VOICE TO GET THE ATTENTION I NEEDED.

- THERE WERE MANY BABIES IN THE ORPHANAGE. THE HELPERS USED STRING, TIED TO OUR WRISTS AND TO OUR CRIBS, TO MAKE CERTAIN WE DIDN'T FALL AND GET HURT. WHEN I WAS A BABY, I HAD A MARK ON MY WRIST FROM THE STRING. THE HELPERS WANTED TO BE SURE I AND THE OTHER CHILDREN WERE SAFE.

- MY BIRTH MOTHER WAS PARENTING SIX YOUNG CHILDREN WITHOUT ANY HELP. SOMETIMES SHE WENT TO WORK IN TOWN SO SHE WOULD HAVE MONEY TO BUY FOOD FOR US. THE SOCIAL WORKER SAID THAT I SOOTHED MYSELF BY SINGING LITTLE SONGS WHILE MY BIRTH MOTHER WAS GONE, AND I FELT WORRIED OR LONELY. THIS HELPED ME FEEL BETTER UNTIL SHE RETURNED.

- I WAS PLACED NEXT TO A BENCH AT A TRAIN STATION. THIS BUSY SPOT MUST HAVE BEEN CHOSEN SO THAT SOMEONE WOULD FIND ME RIGHT AWAY.

- WHEN I LIVED IN THE ORPHANAGE, MY CLOTHING WAS WORN. EVEN THOUGH THEY DIDN'T HAVE NEW OR EXTRA CLOTHING THERE, I COULD TELL FROM THE NUMBER OF TIMES MY CLOTHES WERE RESEWN THAT THE NANNIES TRIED VERY HARD TO PROVIDE FOR THE NEEDS OF THE CHILDREN.

- SINCE THE AUNTIES HAD MANY CHILDREN TO TAKE CARE OF, THEY WEREN'T ABLE TO GIVE US ALL OF THE INDIVIDUAL ATTENTION WE NEEDED. I LEARNED TO COMFORT MYSELF BY GENTLY SUCKING ON MY TONGUE. IN THIS WAY, I COULD COMFORT MYSELF WHENEVER I WANTED IT, EVEN WHEN THE AUNTIES WERE NOT AVAILABLE.

Barbara, a workshop participant, shared the following example which illustrates the use of positive reframing in the course of play: Barbara's three-year-old daughter, Zoey, who was born in Russia, guides her in pretend play. In the story, the birth mother throws her child away in the ocean, and the baby is saved by her adoptive mother.

By reframing the scenario to include the birth mother making a thoughtful plan for her daughter (as her birth mother, reportedly, clearly had), the birth mother was presented in a more positive light and the adoptive mother was removed from the (unhealthy) role of rescuer. This revised version highlights her birth mother's strengths: "The birth mother gets into a boat with the baby and rows to a very special place, where the adoptive family would meet them."

EXERCISE 9 · *Positive Reframing*

Part 1: Identifying the "hard parts"
What do you imagine to be challenging aspects of your child's story to share with her?

_____

_____

_____

_____

_____

_____

_____

_____

_____

_____

_____

_____

_____

_____

_____

_____

_____

_____

_____

_____

Part 2: Naming her strengths
What were some of the strengths demonstrated by your child, or her birth parents, in the situations you presented in Part 1? How might you build on these strengths to reframe the story in a more positive light?

_____

_____

_____

_____

_____

_____

_____

_____

_____

_____

_____

_____

_____

_____

_____

_____

_____

_____

_____

CHAPTER 4

How to Use Your Child's Lifebook

How to Use Your Child's Lifebook

I T IS IMPORTANT to share a child's story with her from the time she is young, repeating concepts introduced earlier and gradually building upon them. By responding to their children's inquiries and planting seeds of information over time, parents build a connection for their children to their pasts.

By the time children are able to understand the contents of their lifebooks, many have been introduced, at some level, to all of the information it contains. As questions, feelings, and thoughts arise, your child can refer to her lifebook as a source of information. A lifebook can serve as an effective launching point for further discussion as well. While sharing in your child's book with her, connections can be drawn between the text, conversations you have had together, and new thoughts.

A child's lifebook should be easy for her to access. It may be viewed as one cherished, tangible place where she can find the facts of her early life. Your child may or may not choose to share it with you, or others, at different times in her emotional development. Alternatively, she may not show interest in her lifebook now; however, she will look to it when she is ready.

Parents tend to value the practice they receive as lifebook composers. As children approach them with questions, parents often find themselves referring back, in their minds, to the framework of that particular concept in the lifebook. Their words, they report, then flow more easily.

One parent, Lorraine, shared the following: Her six-year-old daughter, Olivia, was asked by a friend about visiting China, her country of origin, some day with her adoptive family. Olivia replied that she and her family are not permitted to travel there since her family includes two children, which violates a rule in China. Lorraine sought to clarify China's family policy for Olivia, explaining that it would not prohibit their family from visiting. Lorraine attributed her ability to comfortably respond to Olivia, in part, to her experience creating her lifebook.

Establishing personal boundaries

"IS IT OK FOR MY DAUGHTER TO BRING HER LIFEBOOK TO SCHOOL?"

My daughter, at age six, was playing among statues in a city plaza. She moved from statue to statue, tapping each on the sleeve, asking typical questions one might hear from a passerby: "Excuse me, do you have the time?" "Excuse me, can you tell me how to get to the library?" "Excuse me, where is your child from?" Apparently it seemed just as natural to her to hear the latter question as the others. Children in multiracial and multicultural adoptive families are often asked well-meaning yet intrusive questions about their lives. Parents strive to help them define their personal boundaries so they will learn when to share their backgrounds and with whom. Some of this is achieved through modeling.

Lifebooks are intimate chronicles of our children's early lives. In their younger years, our guidance can help them determine with whom their lifebooks might be shared, just as it helps them with other personal limits. A five-year-old may want to share her lifebook at a neighborhood function, but a thirteen-year-old may think it intrusive if neighbors know the personal details of her early life.

Some parents have wondered how to respond to the inquiries of an older sister or brother who is curious about a younger child's personal beginnings. There are ways to provide older siblings with general information, omitting the individual details that make her story unique. Consider allowing your child to make the decisions to share specific knowledge of her personal beginnings, with your guidance, of course, along the way.

Lifebooks contain intimate information that needs to be treated with special care. Children learn from parents (from both deliberate teaching and modeling) what and how much of their beginnings to share. The intricacies of our children's pasts belong to them; as their parents, we need to handle the personal nature of this information and its meaning to our children with the utmost respect.

CHAPTER 5

Final Thoughts

FINAL THOUGHTS

HAVING SPOKEN ABOUT lifebooks with many groups of parents, and after having created lifebooks for my children and children for whom I am professionally responsible, I feel certain that much of the lifebook work happens prior to the writing. This workbook often refers to the process of creating the lifebook and the subsequent benefits to parents. It is my professional and personal experience that the bulk of these benefits occurs not while consciously working on the book, but rather when a bit of information just sits with us, mildly simmering, and we think about it or try it on, in different ways, over time.

I suggest that parents allow themselves room to "sit" on their child's beginnings for a while, without demanding of themselves the timely creation of the lifebook "product." If you allow yourself some time up front, it's likely to be reflected later in the quality of the book and in your discussions with your child.

Let's return for a moment to the four concepts of this approach to lifebooks highlighted earlier:

1. Adoptive families are one of many variations of strong and healthy families.
2. The stories of our children's beginnings belong to them. They need the truth. We sensitively and honestly reframe information for them to emphasize their resilience and strengths. Our children are then able to view their own beginnings from this positive orientation.

3. Parents develop greater competence and confidence by preparing their children's lifebooks. We become less afraid to talk with our children about their beginnings. We are better able to welcome their thoughts, feelings, questions, and discussion.

4. In many areas, the community of adoptive parents is accessible and well-organized. Parents can look to one another for support and encouragement as they prepare and document their children's beginnings.

Some of the lifebook workshop groups have arranged subsequent meetings to support and encourage one another while creating their children's lifebooks. Consider organizing a group in your community in which parents can meet to discuss talking with their children about adoption or to brainstorm how one might positively reframe particular scenarios presented by the group members. In addition to sharing with and learning from one another, it can be reassuring to know others who have had thoughts, feelings, and experiences similar to your own.

We prepare our children to take care of themselves in many ways. We teach them to honor the whole of their identities. We teach our children to be safe, to exercise good judgment, and to trust their inner voices. With lifebooks — a bridge to their beginnings — they are better equipped to rely on their instincts to manage these everyday realities. With a more complete understanding of where they came from and who they are, our children stand on firmer ground.

"MOM, I THINK THE NAME *LIFEBOOK*
SHOULD BE CHANGED TO *LIFESAVER*."
– *Julie, age 8*

RECOMMENDED READING

BROWN, JANE. "What do we tell them?" *Adoption Today Magazine*, May 2000.

SARA DOROW, editor. *I Wish for You a Beautiful Life*. Minnesota: Yeong and Yeong Book Company, 1999.

JOHNSON, KAY. *Wanting a Daughter, Needing a Son*. Minnesota: Yeong and Yeong Book Company, 2004.

MELINA, LOIS. "Adoptive parents must overcome concerns to convey difficult information to adoptees." *Adopted Child*. Vol. 16:10. October 1997.

MELINA, LOIS. "Parents advised of ways to explain abandonment to children." *Adopted Child*. Vol. 15:2. February 1996.

PIPHER, MARY. *The Shelter of Each Other – Rebuilding our Families*. New York: G.P. Putnam's Sons, 1996.

PROBST, CINDY. "Adoption lifebooks: With so many how-to's, how do you choose?" *Adoptive Families,* January/February 2001.

REGISTER, CHERI. "Answering nosy questions: help your children respond in appropriate ways." *Adoptive Families,* July/August 1994.

VONK, ELIZABETH M. "Cultural competence for transracial adoptive parents." *Social Work,* July 2001.

WARD, JANIE VICTORIA. *The Skin We're In*. New York: The Free Press, 2000.